TO BOYS WITH GREEN HAIR

TO BOYS WITH GREEN HAIR

Arthur Jackson V

A Rebel Satori Imprint

New Orleans

Published in the United States of America by
REBEL SATORI PRESS
www.rebelsatori.com

Contents

To Boys With Green Hair

I stole morning
For a glass of wine
;I wanted to drown out the sound
I pictured myself a green haired boy

My reflection chimed "you aren't held in
                              Passion, fever, or want"

Hiding my insecurities
In a cage fashioned from my ribs
I said "one day you will be worthy"

I still remember the sun
Setting horizon beneath my wrist
That night I huffed
A volcano bottlenecking my throat

When we lei together grapes&weeds
And called them crowns
We adorned our heads

I clasped to clench palms kneading
Their heels to wet eyes
Thinking of He and I

The sky and trees all

Beautiful like the day
We first learned to see

It was The Summer of Love
you told me not to speak
This shows me whether
in lustwords we
Would always be at war

Must a kiss be sent over soot
aimed between us?

A piece of me is lost
It is loaded
bottled by the wine
Left to puffing cumulus whales along sky
I bend my neck back
Smoke howls at the moon

I passionned for your want
You called it starving

We weren't loving over wargrounds
For sooted kisses

Signals smoked from a volcano
Bottlenecking my throat

I tried to forget you
In sips
You forgot me in hales

We both lost our crowns
wailing under sunset on our backs
In grass that stained our hair
And I became a Banshee

Green Out of Necessity

Remember when we contorted ourselves
around eachother?   Ripened grapevines –
Your eyes made wine of me. I didn't
[don't] mind
the bending, in fact I love it!

I so miss being green; the grandeur of your twist.
I forfeit to stand tall of leaves
(you, i) and
vines – those grapes and ripen
Soon, again, you'll make wine
then, I'll be that wine
A perse budding from stem

There won't be this cork harboring
us a stopper
Keeping us bottled
sour adolescence
picked out of season
for bitter taste buds

Was the Sound Green?

I am conflicted
I'm conflicted
I've been conned
I've been flicked
There is an irritant
Your words are thieves
With hidden knives
In back pockets
We had a forest once
But too true   Alysia called out
Words for their alphabet of cutlery

Remember the green?
The living sound?

A past love white
knuckled syllable value
This left us silent
I was preferred in'silent
He too collected sharpeneds
And the sounds left by trees
Upon fall without audience

Horcrux

"I want to be a tangle of sheets & legs again"

All of me wanted
To find you
On your bed   In
Your old worn white robe
Cheekbones bloating with smiles

Warm&waiting   for me
A ps4 wireless controller extends
The length your hand

I remember trading face crossing
White Spreads for anecdote
To calm the flight pattern
Of butterflies migrating between
My head and gut;
Of course, it never worked

I used to press my nose
To your armpits   Deep inhale
Your scent where most pure
Incase we while'd space

I haven't seen you in a while

The Eventide

Once, you showed me
I have stars bottle-necked in my throat
and called night the Eventide

I wonder if you've forgotten
Our language, beyond The night
we inhaled applewood   .I remember
your words
you signed them along my lips

Your calligraphy has embers
&savoures of the morning
summer left us
in pieces

We had bonfire-love,
fags of apple wood
burn in our necks
When we kiss
we eat to the core

Some'boy's smoking
in the window seal
making tea of his tears
The smoke and steam take
the shape of stars

Reminiscent of the night
You tossed red giants

Sometimes,
I speak of embers in my sleep
'Bout how
an apple made like sugar
in my throat
&stars fell from night
A rubious rain

at a party I drank myself
Into a wobbling horizon&
asked you to kiss me instead
you whispered poems
against my mouth
sprouting roots
From my tongue

Now-a-nights,
I trace your face in the tideless sky
'cause hands remember
Cerebral artists
kept track record
the angles of your face
Your face like
a double edged sword
I've since learned love
Like yours begs
with a warning label

In January you left me
with tears I boiled for tea
It was the easiest way
I could remember the taste
of an ache

When you took up
a handful of stars
from my throat
looking into my eyes
A try to make wine
&called me the Eventide
Then tossed the stars
An offering to sky
Night

It came quickly and left
as fast as a Flame
before morning embers
behind horizon
we left pieces
after gorging on apples

When we kiss
It taste like fire

Star shards

Not every landscape begs
A photograph   A golden light
Blankets for everyone

Everything becomes Eldorado

Royal cloak of morning
Below trailing tutti like birth
-right.

I wonder if you ever snuck
A photo of me like I did
Of you   Pollen is a flowers
Memento to the soil   Even when
Milk and honey run dry

A silken thread seams silver linings
To clouds   A bag I'd given
You – now, with a fixing stitch
I didn't weave with needle

Were we a series of return to
   Sender?

Do you remember teaching me
To write a perfect letter? You said "a good letter

Will get your want"
But, threw my words at my face
Post mark the date by
My papercut stare   Maybe I should've
Stamped the top right edge red
So we could scab over

Is this how love comes
To stammer? Blood
Gushing out and no one
To say I'm sorry?

Even stars shard golden light
Then tinge red before going out

When Naming The Event Horizon

I like your lips
Your lips on my lips
be it—when astrologists named
the outside of a black hole
were they speaking sweet nothings in
too, [the universe] breathing
Stars in air
On exhale—first light

When you speak my name
there is morning on your breath

How Questions Ache (The Green Shadow)

"Why are you following me?"
"What do you mean?"
My eyes fall into the empty space—starring where he punched a
black hole before me. /Following you?/ it echoes in my head. I
didn't want to get lost in space; I wanted to come back ready with
aim. There I found a question in the event horizon.
You're always there when I turn around . . .
He feels I'm his shadow.
"So often, you call me your shadow, but do you ever stop and think
maybe I'm just drawn to you? Naturally pulled because I find you
intriguing, handsome, easy to talk to, and love you?"

Isn't this what happens in lovers space? Doesn't gravity pull you that
way?

"I never thought about it that way" Gravity didn't pull him that
way. I should have known then to stop watching so long with rose
irises and blushing pupils.
But, I now know how lessons linger before becoming learned.

My eyes walked his sun so, they wore footprints in his surface the
way your head imprints your favorite pillow or light bleaches a
photograph . . . /He must have felt it/ I thought. Maybe all that
starring is what makes love so blinding, afterall overstimulation is
wearing. Can a black hole swallow a sun, so, we don't have to Ache
such questions?

Twin Flame

It's about 9:40pm
Not yet wrapping on twilight
                    I'm warm with
3 quarters of a bottle of Argentina's
finest Malbec;   it's got me yearning
press of your chest into
the broken frame placed
to temporary the hollow left: he, strutting off
with my chest
                    He's accumulated 25&26 Jack

Weebling my entrance
to the local strip mall
mind—3 times drowned
                    in wine— set
on baking the Best Apple Pie, this
also conjures you to mind
all cinnamon & brown sugar caramelized

My twin flame

I baked for him,   so tricked
out of my soul for
The food,   My spine
a fragile spin of scorched sugar
That first burn

14

he gave with /I love you /

Selflove : the best dough is kneaded
                    A practice
Less worth my kitchen magik
My spoon, and fork
His pocket knife, handled like
two adolescent boys in an ally
over a heart

I owe you an apology
I'll lay the words a lattice weave &
brush the tops with an egg
—wash the kinked strips
              for the flakey layers
Capture our roux—
thick with our language
I can hear you love
as opens the oven
The first time
«tu me manque» can't express
the degree of miss

A Sweet Sort of Choking

I left rose quartz
on your window
after you claim it healed you
It no longer manes my neck

The first boy to say
I love you left me wailing
A hummingbird smelled me
then called you a ghost
that veil of smoke keeps us separate

Writing with a lavender quill
Each word
a fragrant rhythm
on a scratch of sheet music
I watched you compose a play enamored
and planted a lavender sprig
in my belly
hoping the scent draw you
There you grow nigh

You once inquest   we
fall asleep with lips arrest
In a kiss; the first time
I tasted lavender on your lips
There we slept like on a bed of roses

Whether lavender or
Lust on our locked tongues—
What a slow way of choking

The first time you said
/I love you / I paced
Roses bottlenecked
in my throat
From bud to bloom, I
questioned its truth

That night we danced
a dancing happy like fire
two flames fund a ghostship
                    devoured
All drywood between us

But we forgot to carry the quartz
with our dancing feet before
locking tongues for restful sleep
The sweet scent lavender left
on me
given my lips
roses bloom in your nigh
A slow kind of choking

Sugar Tales

You're drying up and
down my skin – contraband
scribbled on my forearms
That kiss you laced with smoke
Hot smoke dripped down Castro in heaps
Dressed in Drag
and wet with sailors
I remember thinking
How'd you leave me weak why
Did I let you get away with
Damage

I wish I had a picture saved
A reminder for no return

So done I
back traced your palm-lines by memory
Called it clinical research
the lines leave me circled
Of four swallows
I attempt to read them like runes
A telling throw of gifted fingers
Along love tended alter

But, see, when my head went
I guess he got that too

It /always/ hurts like glass
I feel like the sound of shatter

Shatter You fall-apart
like leaves under feet
rigid Fall
then crunch like autumn
When we were just kids
after hunting hot sugar
Grasping with cold hands
Remember those cavities   The sweetness
Honey sucks where memories of you stem
I can pick them ,the smell
Even still makes the sharp edges
Of my lips
curve a reach for my ears

Finally Uncoiling

My heartbeat felt affections premier
On the back of your wings

When you came back
You lay like warm laundry
Fresh from the dryer. Stoic
With heat

a silent clad of familiar nest

(Something like coming home
On finish of a Monday that reeks
Of Monday
to the smell of baking)

Honey butter caramelizes your exhale

I couldn't conjure words so,settled
for warming your grimace with eager lips

Your eyes made like sugar on mine
Your fingers found the coiled follicles
behind my left ear&
kneaded the scent of a Monday
Fading to night
with four fingers

5 of Pentacles

"The 5 of Pentacles is not a particularly happy indicator when it comes to love questions, unfortunately. You may have your eye on someone who you feel is not treating you the way they should. It may be that you need to stop fantasizing about this person entirely. . . remember that there is never only one person that we can be with and have a soul-level, happy, meaningful relationship. When love is right, you don't have to do backflips to make it work."

In the Leo season
I tried cinnamon to conjure heat
maybe soon after, passion
Though we lacked kindling
So, I was patient a while
A lion's roar singes
it's way up the spine
after a ferocious bite
burning a hole in my pocket
A leo stubbornness that bitters the tongue
My intentions were seasoned
with shavings of the deep parts of me
Set to bake
35 minutes later it left
the oven a savoure I never kneaded

I could taste tampering notes
The base; concrete Medusa eyes – What shooting sight

How you turn to stone when asked
/*how does a lover show it with their back turned?*/
Nothing's all black and white
But, maybe a little less
grey the next

Residuum

A gully
brought into fruition
by erosion

&Forbidden Fruits
seen corroding
teach us etiquette

When first we spoke
I stole
a pomegranate from your tree
It corrodes   once
I eat it

at the edge of a gully
In your patience
I read how

/warmth has potential here/

Huge with our words'we
speaking in circles   recite
 for each other
4 sonnets

I'd go to the moon

for you
Did&took of the sphere
two pieces warm
in my hands
before they cooled

I was loving you a poem
with pomegranate lips-
-slick, now sediment,   they too,
current at the soles
of my feet

I'm thinking of a boy
seeing The Moon; two pieces
of the giant
cooling his hands
Standing in a gully   ,there
reciting himself
how, after picking a perse corpse
it still warms his throat

The last we spoke
You called me a thief

A piece of me sediments
at the bottom of a gully
after corroding

The boy is reciting to no one
how the last bite
of a ruby fruit

sweetens erosion

My body wants
to be the dry-land you edge
;still warm in the place
we serenaded a sedimenting gully
        to fruition

There, a pomegranate
in a tree
looks down where a boy
tipped toes- a reach
for its nape
with warm hands

When last I saw you
I offered a pomegranate
You said "tastes better
, for you" and peeled
back the skin

I ate a pomegranate
It corrodes in my throat
Sedimenting our sonnets

My body—
corpse still warm before
cool

Here, in a gully   ,once
huge with our words

Sonnets circle — how they
became sediment
&we commence
erosion

Song Bird, Banshee, or Nocturnal Creature?

Start of September,   a
89 degree weather night in rem
I saw myself four corners deep
In attempt to invoke
Your love   ,post
August solar eclipse

You, four edges of a room I don't exist
in, but, cannot escape
Imagine a cage
forged from jacks things   My things
[this wabi sabi portrait renders me immure – shaped by lovers
          hands]
Caught by amour; eye averting tricks
          cirrostratus
I've started singing
so stop my tears   Fingers
stained of witches rings
Silver bands – one for each repetition
It seems to calm the withdrawals
reminding your other nocturnal lovers
of lacked sleep
Fatigued burdens with a'mort
          real love   locked at the backs
of their throats
I, even I

Choke to conjure along incantation
I still see their lips singing along

Banshee [Lament for an Ache]

a year ago,   two
Birds calm a branch
Nipping each others shoulders
This leaves them humming

Ce nuit, on écoute un chantant Banshee

And eyes play planchette
To the ouija night

Il se lève   He wakes
In sharp gasps about old
scars becoming inflamed the level
his nape

A red burning in haste
Encourages a hearts beating pace
Beneath a clavicle trellis

A parallel race over
Befor'tasted marrow par
Les épaules

Banchèe with A New Song

I've been told my words purr
with loss
When you plant a seed   intent
assumed growth – infuse that plotted earth
Nourish thirst with kind language
An indigo child I call brother once said
"/speak love into my air/" I wish
Days for days weren't so distracting

I have a Twin Flame she
Taught me "/always with intention/"
But distraction and a bruise—
Easily—pride stole
The lesson in a glass box

The plot runs dry
Leaves shatter breaking fall
What beautiful green we
Could've spread for gardens

Two hands are covered in dirt

Call Back Melody

"You watch someone long enough, and you can see their humanity"

A chorus of Banshees
sing in low octaves
the farewell blues

Have you ever wanted
to love all up on someone
so much
your heart complains about
the upstairs neighbors
that constant noise

Juxtaposed vibrations - call back conversation
Wilde thumpa thumpa of deep house
        to my hoppy jazz, often improvisation imagine

Walking at 3:00am
Bring it Back
Moloko on high a strut
alongside Take 5
Jerreau sipping stomped aged grapes

Tu Me Manque

I'll attempt to live 'morrow as
never you left
art a broken frame of canvas
post attempt
demons bite and jump; lungs wretch
ribs contract off your venom
Tears fall like in love with hurricanes

Two lovers end twice

Love deters in your exiting shadow
And ,yet ,stubbornly remains
Un jour, je trouverai un sourire
un propagation sauvage à travers ma visage
et, le compterai trois fois

City Living [rolled stogues with sage]

Around midnight on 19th
& Taraval
Three different sides pulled together
angles from tears
Natural causes have nothing to do
with tonight's rain
Just your usual San Francisco trifferie
worth its weight in bills
starved for those due
being told it's not enough
Relationships who can't
speak the same language
especially when midnight
has brought rum alongside
Tonight has palpable notes
of insecurity where prayers
for security are hummed in intense silence
Can you hear them?
Crying for morning
crying for light   , attempting trade
of hiccoughs for clarity
Sitting on the stoop
smoking rolled stogues
with sage
Sediment in the night

And What of the Gardener

He punk'boy smokes spirits   While walking
leaves his scent behind
because eating smoke is more
Chanel than eating dust

Wanting to belong to a good time

At 4:20 he wants to hit 440
but remembers how they watched
as he teased me from my body
and left a corps
I wonder if he's still wet-with-himself?

Is this how flowers scream
when picked?
In odd frequencies and dusted with pollen

Ode for Haight&Clayton [Blue Dream Spliff] [American Spirits Nonfiltered]

One night
in rarely warm
midtown San Francisco
we lifted your past
barehanded into the near
now of Haight&Clayton

We sat on your stoop
per stogue
you spoke
voice softer than
warranted the passing weekend
We talked about art
laughed intimately
in spite our exhaustion
Labored chests, that too
we salvaged

Spectrum

My favorite part
about driving into a city
are the lights you see
from the freeway
Upon entry
You don't see people
just clusters
of colored lights
like God decided
we're in need
of a bit of heaven
and took up two
handfuls of stars
tossing them
into a plane

(I think of you)

I don't live here
but, I come often
for the lights
and clusters of color
washing over me a spectrum
warm reds and yellows
cool blues and greens
tinting the skin

I belong to them
even if temporarily

(yours)

I don't live here
but, I come often
and you wash over me

The Salinity of Ocean Park

This is what leaving
San Francisco looks like
but, I'm back now   ,and
coming home flown me over
tidal pools
A congregation of colored water masses
          Tinged by salt ;Microorganisms
—they prefer *Microalgae*
Color determined of tolerant
for salinity   This spectrum
made arriving   *Ocean Park*
Landing strip laid by Diebencorn
          —Bay air seasoned of Matisse
Salinity conjures language on the tongue
An easy sprout

Cumulus

It would be my undoing
To fall through the sun-slit
of a cumulus, brilliant
where it is most dense
Sometimes you cross my mind
and the L goes silent
The robust clouds towered
over two people on a bench
contemplating skin
but first with lips
Supple and pulls me like the wind
pulls the clouds

Walking at 3am

always a silent quest   we trek
Chelsea boots strut—signs of leatherwear
heels clack to the rhythmic timbre
murmurs to empty streets
a high ties line 'round my head
I'm weeble wobbly
it's got me spitting shushed chuckles   ,but
you can't hear
you've got your headphones on and,
the city is silent
we pass doorways   ,clad
with a trim of faces

mimics of renaissance reliefs.they
look like they want to speak
but the city is so quiet
my heart is eager

a shouting almost palpable

but suffice wait on cities wake
I don't want to shatter
San Francisco's fragile silence   It's just
small window – I'll wait
you might not be wearing headphones then, and
I'll have found the language
Lips aimed with Read

CPSIA information can be obtained
at www.ICGtesting.com
Printed in the USA
LVHW111210140720
660655LV00002B/102

9 781608 641390